DISCOVER HAWAI'I'S FRESHWATER WILDLIFE

BY KATHERINE ORR

Hawaiian Islands National Wildlife Refuge

Midway Atoll National Wildlife Refuge

Kure Atoll
(State Sanctuary)

Pearl and Hermes Atoll

Northwestern Ha

Laysan Island

Maro Reef

Lisianski Island

Gardner Pinnacles

French Frigate Shoals

PACIFIC

DISCOVER HAWAI'I'S FRESHWATER WILDLIFE

Written and illustrated by Katherine Orr

Originally published by

ISLAND HERITAGE
PUBLISHING
A DIVISION OF THE MADDEN CORPORATION

Reprinted in 2020 by Katherine Orr with permission from Island Heritage.
For eductionl use.
Please address orders and correspondence to:

Katherine Orr
44-119 Bayview Haven Place.
Kaneohe, HI 96744, USA
(808) 234-5508 www.katherineshelleyorr.com

Copyright © 2020 by Katherine S. Orr
All rights reserved. Portions of this book may be reproduced and modified for educational purposes with permission from the author.
Printed in the USA

Discover
Hawai'i's FRESHWATER
Wildlife

Written and Illustrated
by Katherine Orr

Contents

Introduction 3
Where fresh water comes from 4
Plants are part of the freshwater system 5
Water shapes the land 6
Hawai'i's stream-climbers 8
    Where do stream-climbers come from? 9
    Stream gobies, or 'o'opu 10
    Shrimp, or 'opae 16
    Climbing snails, or hīhīwai 18
Other stream wildlife 19
    Limnaeid snails 19
    Insects 20
Estuaries 22
Wetlands 24
Hawai'i's waterbirds 25
Visiting waterbirds 32
Waterbirds in danger 34
People and freshwater 36
The future is in our hands 40
How You Can Help 41
Glossary 42
Index 43

Introduction

Fresh water paints a silver thread against the mountain as it falls. It tumbles down through leafy forests, swirls in deep pools, and rushes on across dark boulders. As it nears the ocean, the stream slows. Its waters spread out among marshes—where it is used by people and by crops—until, at last, it joins the sea.

There is beauty in these waterfalls, pools, and marshes—and much more. On a slippery rock behind the waterfall, young Hawaiian fish are climbing up, inch by inch, against the pounding flow. Within a deep pool, Hawaiian shrimps dart quickly to escape the jaws of foreign invaders. Among the marsh ponds, a Hawaiian duck leads her newly hatched ducklings out to feed.

Hawai'i's freshwater streams and wetlands are home to wildlife that are found nowhere else in the world. The story of how these animals live and how they got here begins with the story of fresh water.

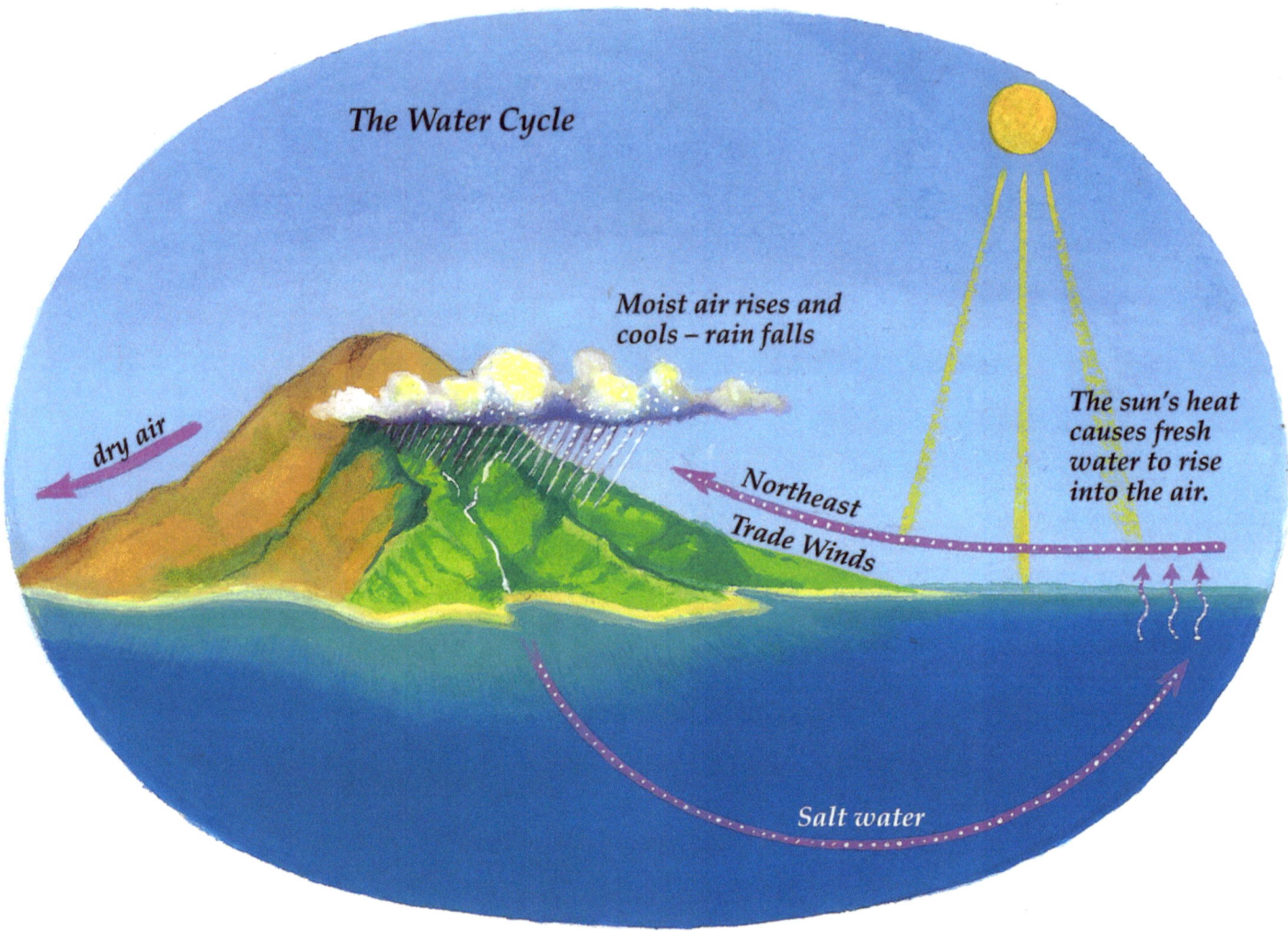

WHERE FRESH WATER COMES FROM

The fresh water of Hawai'i's streams and wetlands comes from the ocean as part of a great cycle that shapes the land and feeds all life. As the sun warms the surface of the ocean and the layer of air over it, some water rises into the air as tiny droplets of moisture. This warm, moist air blows across Hawai'i's islands in a steady flow from the northeast, called the trade winds. As the air blows toward the mountains, it is forced to rise. Rising up the mountain slopes to a higher altitude, the air cools. Cool air cannot carry as much moisture as hot air. As it runs into the mountains, the rising, cooling air forms clouds that release the moisture as rain. The far sides of the mountains stay dry because the air drops most of its moisture on the windward side. Sometimes, very warm, wet, air blows toward Hawai'i from the southwest. When this air cools, it drops lots of rain on the south, or "Kona," side of the islands. During these Kona storms, ten or twenty inches of rain may fall in less than a day, causing flash floods.

PLANTS ARE PART OF THE FRESHWATER SYSTEM

When rain falls on the land, some water soaks into the ground, some is taken up by plants, some flows into streams, and some returns to the air as tiny droplets of moisture. In the high mountain forests, plants help bring more water to the land. Water from the moist air collects on millions of leaves and drips to the ground. Trees shade out the sun, keeping the air and soil in the high forests cool and damp. Rotting plants mix with the soil and help it hold moisture, like a sponge. Roots and fallen leaves hold the soil in place during heavy rains. In these ways, plants help bring fresh water to the land and hold it there.

The roots of plants that grow alongside streams and in marshlands— soft, wet, low-lying land—help hold soil in place, while their stems and leaves slow the speed of raging flood waters. As flowing water slows down, it drops much of the soil it was carrying. Thus, plants help keep precious soil on the land, while also keeping the ocean and streams clean. Rains and floods wash dead leaves and other plant materials into streams, where flowing water grinds them into bits. These small particles feed stream animals such as insects, shrimps, and baby fish.

Mountain forests help fresh water return to plants, ground, and streams. Without forests, rainwater would rush down steep slopes to the sea, washing away soil and leaving the ground dry.
Silt and soil smother coral reefs. By helping to keep soil from being washed to the sea, plants help coral reefs survive.

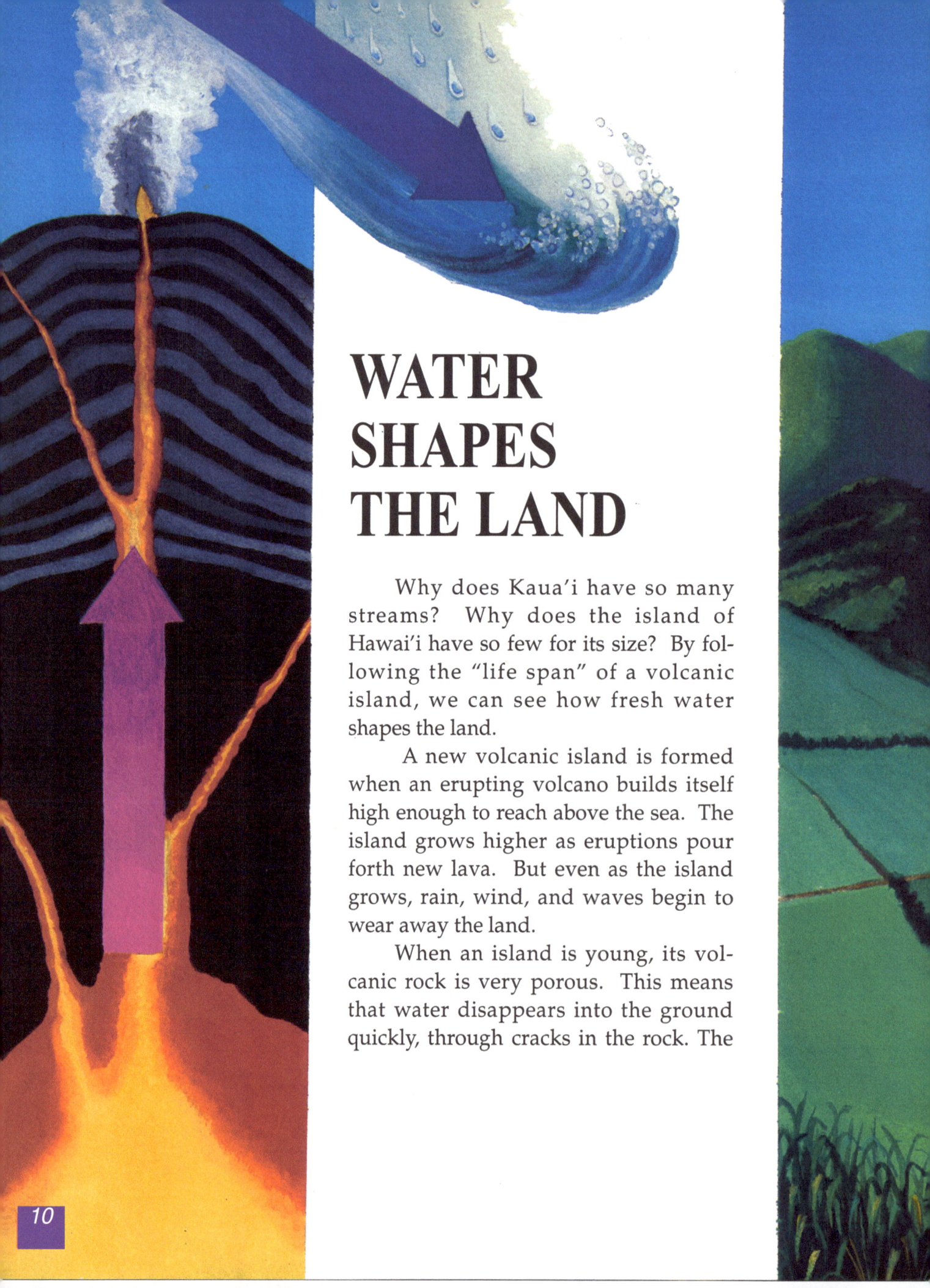

WATER SHAPES THE LAND

Why does Kaua'i have so many streams? Why does the island of Hawai'i have so few for its size? By following the "life span" of a volcanic island, we can see how fresh water shapes the land.

A new volcanic island is formed when an erupting volcano builds itself high enough to reach above the sea. The island grows higher as eruptions pour forth new lava. But even as the island grows, rain, wind, and waves begin to wear away the land.

When an island is young, its volcanic rock is very porous. This means that water disappears into the ground quickly, through cracks in the rock. The

island of Hawai'i is the youngest Hawaiian island. Its newest land has no streams because all the rainwater that falls there soaks into the ground and drains away beneath the surface.

As an island ages, the chemical and physical effects of wind, rain, and plants turn the volcanic rock into clay and soil. Forests and streams develop, and flowing water changes the shape of the land. Over millions of years, streams and rivers carve the mountains into sharp ridges and deep valleys. Rivers carry sand, gravel, and soil to their mouths, where flat marshlands are built up near the sea. Kaua'i has more streams than Hawai'i's other high islands because it is the oldest high island in the Hawaiian chain. Kaua'i's steep, wrinkled mountains, as well as its deep valleys and canyons, have been shaped by flowing water that wears away the land. Some day, the island of Hawai'i will have steep, wrinkled mountains and many streams—just like Kaua'i.

HAWAI'I'S STREAM-CLIMBERS

Steep land and heavy mountain rains create interesting streams that are always changing. Most Hawaiian streams are steep and small. They form lively stretches of shallow rapids, slippery waterfalls, and deep pools. They can become raging floods that rise several feet within minutes and then return to their normal flow within hours. Sometimes their course even changes if the flood carves out new pathways. Some streams dry up at times, while a few never reach the sea at all!

What animals live in these streams and how did they get here? Scientists have found some interesting answers. Hawai'i's most unusual stream animals are a group of fish, shrimps, and snails that spend their adult lives in fresh water, but produce young that need to live at sea. Their eggs hatch in freshwater streams, but the hatchlings are quickly washed downstream to the ocean. After weeks or months of drifting in the ocean, the young fish, shrimps, and snails find their way back to Hawai'i's streams. Many begin a long journey upstream, even climbing up the faces of high waterfalls, to reach their new homes. Some of these stream-climbers are able to climb waterfalls that pour down cliffs directly into the sea!

Where Do Stream-Climbers Come From?

Plants and animals can only come to Hawai'i by air or by sea. So, how did life move into Hawai'i's freshwater streams when the Hawaiian Islands are surrounded by hundreds of miles of salty ocean? Scientists believe that, over many generations, certain saltwater fish, shrimps, and snails that lived in shallow seas near shore evolved, or changed, in ways that allowed them to live in freshwater streams. The adults became able to live only in fresh water, but their larvae (LAR-vee), or young, remained able to live only in the sea. This unusual lifestyle allows these animals to spread from one stream to another, carried by ocean currents when they are young.

Scientists think stream-climbers first developed on other, older, Pacific islands. After the Hawaiian Islands were formed, a few of these young fish, shrimps, and snails drifted here on ocean currents and moved up Hawaiian streams. Over many generations, they evolved into forms better suited to live in Hawai'i's steep, flashy, streams. Over time, most of them have become Hawai'i's own fish, shrimps, and snails, found nowhere else on earth.

Stream gobies

Hawai'i's five native freshwater fish are called stream gobies, or *'o'opu-wai*. Four of these five kinds of fish are true gobies. True gobies have a sucker, or suction cup, on their underside, formed by two fins joined together. Stream gobies use their sucker to cling to the bottom of rushing streams and climb up waterfalls. The fifth fish is also called an *'o'opu*, but it is not a true goby because it has no sucker.

The suction cup on a goby's belly is formed by two fins that are permanently joined together.

The largest and most common stream goby in Hawai'i is the *'o'opu nakea*. It grows up to fourteen inches long, and can be recognized by its beautiful golden color and stripes on the fins along its back and tail. *'O'opu nakea* are most commonly found in streams mid-way between mountains and sea. They feed mainly on insects and fine, green, water plants called algae (AL-jee), or *limu*. They also eat some snails and earthworms.

'O'opu nakea's life cycle is much like that of other stream gobies. When the streams first swell with rain at the start of the fall rainy season, *'o'opu nakea* swim downstream to mate and lay eggs. The female lays a patch of yellow eggs on a rock in the stream. The eggs stick to the rock, and the male fertilizes them by covering the eggs with his sperm. One or both male and female guard the eggs until they hatch, about twenty-four hours later.

The newly hatched *'o'opu nakea* larvae wash downstream to the ocean. There is no time to lose, because *'o'opu* larvae cannot survive for long in fresh water. They must reach the ocean quickly or die. By laying eggs only during

'O'opu nakea

times of heavy rain, when Hawai'i's streams are full and rushing, 'o'opu parents help give their young a speedy ride to the sea.

Once in the ocean, the larvae join millions of other tiny animals and plants that drift in the sea. These drifting plants and animals are called "plankton." Nearly every drop of sea water has some plankton in it. Plankton is a very important source of food for life in the ocean.

'O'opu larvae are carried by ocean currents along the coast, sometimes as far

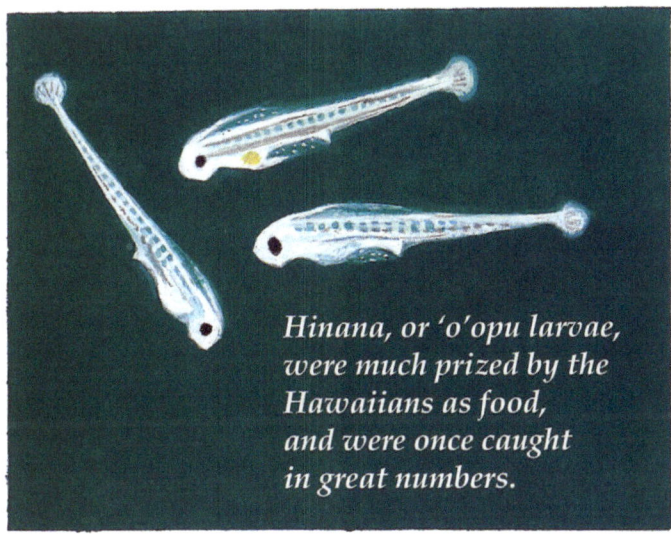

Hinana, or 'o'opu larvae, were much prized by the Hawaiians as food, and were once caught in great numbers.

as other Hawaiian islands. During this time, they eat plankton. Many of the larvae die when they drift too far out to sea or are thrown ashore by waves. Many are eaten by fish and other sea animals. Those that are still alive after four to six months of drifting in the ocean are ready to return to freshwater streams.

Between December and the following July, *'o'opu nakea* larvae enter streams and rivers, working hard to move upstream against the flowing water as it pours into the sea. These *hinana*, as the Hawaiians call all *'o'opu* larvae, have clear bodies and are less than an inch long, yet they are able to swim against the stream's powerful flow. Soon after entering the stream, the young fish develop colors and swim along the bottom, as their parents do. These *ahina* make their way upstream, where they grow into adults and live for the rest of their lives. By clinging to the rocks with their suckers and then wriggling with their tails, they can hold their position in a stream during a storm and even climb up waterfalls.

Once, *hinana* could be found by the millions, entering stream mouths and swimming upstream from the sea. The Hawaiians caught them in enormous numbers for food. Today, because most of Hawai'i's natural streams have been disturbed and damaged, there are much fewer *hinana*. To help keep *'o'opu nakea* in our streams, *hinana* are now protected by law.

Today, adult *'o'opu nakea* are still a popular food. With the first heavy rains of the season, fishermen line the stream banks to catch *'o'opu nakea* for themselves and their families. Because *'o'opu nakea* are not as common as they once were, it is against the law to sell them.

'*O'opu 'alamo'o* is a small goby that grows to six inches long. It lives mainly in the middle and upper parts of Hawai'i's streams, where the water is clear and fast-flowing. It is the best climber of all the gobies, struggling up waterfalls sometimes 300 feet high. Scientists have found these gobies living above a series of six waterfalls, stretching up more than 800 feet!

Unlike *'o'opu nakea*, which often live together in groups, adult male *'o'opu 'alamo'o* are territorial. This means that each male chooses his own patch of stream bottom, or territory, and keeps other males out of it. Within this territory, the male has one or more favorite places to sit—often atop a rock—where he can see small shrimp and other foods drift by, and watch the comings and goings of other fish.

Female *'o'opu 'alamo'o* are a gray-green or yellow-brown color. Males are usually these colors, too, but when a male sees a female swimming into his territory, he quickly changes into breeding colors. In an instant, his front end becomes black and his tail end turns bright red-orange, or orange-white. His bright blue eyes stand out against his black face, and

'O'opu 'alamo'o

Female

Male in courtship colors

his body fins turn white. The male moves toward the female and raises his fins. He curves his body to one side and then the other, showing her his bright colors. Often, the female is not interested in him. As she moves away, the male's bright colors fade. Within several minutes, his colors return to their usual brownish or greenish shades.

When a strange male 'o'opu 'alamo'o passes through another male's territory, the "owner" of the territory changes to a darker shade of breeding colors and swims to meet the stranger. Turning sideways, the owner flicks the first fin on his back up and down. If this fin-flicking doesn't cause the stranger to leave, the owner spreads his fins, grips the bottom with his sucker, and waggles back and forth in a threatening way until the stranger gets his message. As the stranger swims away, the owner follows him to the edge of his territory, flicking his fin or waggling back and forth all the way.

'O'opu 'alamo'o live in streams that are very clean and undisturbed. Unfortunately, because of human activities, few natural, undisturbed streams remain in Hawai'i. As suitable living places for this fish become more scarce, 'o'opu 'alamo'o become more scarce as well.

Young 'O'opu climbing up a water fall.

'O'opu nopili live in clean, fast-flowing streams about mid-way between mountains and sea, slightly upstream of 'o'opu nakea, and downstream of 'o'opu alamo'o. They grow to eight inches long and feed by scraping algae and stream insects from stones. 'O'opu nopili climb straight up very high waterfalls by moving their suckers from side to side as they wriggle up the slippery rocks.

'O'opu nopili

Scientists have watched groups of young 'o'opu climb straight up waterfalls at a rate of eighteen inches in twenty seconds. They have stared in wonder as groups of tiny 'o'opu, dangling by their suckers, moved along the wet ceilings of rock ledges on their journey up the falls. Although scientists have difficulty telling one kind of 'o'opu from another when they are very young, perhaps these dramatic danglers were young 'o'opu 'alamo'o, heading toward a new life in one of Hawai'i's highest, clean streams. Or perhaps they were 'o'opu nopili, the waterfall-climbers that have the strongest suckers of all the gobies.

‘O‘opu naniha

‘O‘opu naniha is a small goby that grows to about six inches long. It has a black stripe below each eye, and a solid gray or tan body that can change quickly to dark stripes. Like *‘o‘opu nakea*, it sometimes hides by burying in sand, with only its eyes showing. Although it has a sucker, *‘o‘opu naniha* doesn't climb waterfalls. It lives only in the lower parts of streams, and at the mouths of streams where fresh water and sea water mix. *‘O‘opu naniha* likes quiet streams, and feeds on small plants and animals by burrowing its nose in the soft, sandy or muddy bottom.

‘O‘opu ‘akupa

‘O‘opu ‘akupa is not a true goby because the fins on its belly are not joined to form a suction cup. It cannot climb waterfalls, and so lives only in the lower parts of streams. It grows up to twelve inches long, and feeds on many stream animals, including other *‘o‘opu*. *‘O‘opu ‘akupa* and *‘o‘opu naniha* can live in disturbed streams that are not so clean, so their existence is probably not as threatened as that of the other *‘o‘opu*.

Mountain Shrimp
'Opae kala-'ole

tiny, pointed legs to climb up waterfalls and along wet mosses and ferns.

'Opae kala-'ole feed by using special front legs with fan-like hairs. Where water is flowing quickly, the shrimps face into the current and catch bits of food that drift into their special leg hairs. First one leg and then the other opens and closes, as each shrimp catches food and brings it to its mouth. Scientists studying mountain streams have come across groups of *'opae kala-'ole* standing shoulder to shoulder, facing upstream with their arms outstretched, feeding. In pools where the water is quiet, *'opae kala-'ole* collect bits of food along the bottom by raking the ground with their leg hairs.

'Opae 'oeha'a live in the lower part of

Shrimp, or *'Opae*

'Opae kala-'ole, or mountain shrimp, live in fast-flowing streams high in the mountains. They grow to be about two inches long, and are often found together in large groups. *'Opae kala-'ole* breed throughout the year. Like all shrimps, female *'opae* carry their eggs underneath the tail until they hatch. Newly hatched shrimp, as small as specks, wash down from mountain streams to the sea, where they drift in the plankton. Ocean currents carry them from one stream mouth to another, and from one island to another. After drifting in the ocean for about three months, the young shrimp enter a stream and crawl to the mountains, using their

A common stream animal that is not native to Hawai'i, is the Tahitian prawn. Humans brought Tahitian prawns to Hawai'i in 1956. Like the 'opae and 'o'opu, its young wash into the sea from streams and are spread along the coast by ocean currents. Within fifteen years of their arrival, Tahitian prawns had moved into nearly every Hawaiian stream that reaches the sea. Tahitian prawns catch many kinds of smaller animals for food, and are caught for food by fishermen. In high mountain streams that are difficult for people to fish, the prawns gather in large numbers and probably eat many 'o'opu and 'opae.

streams and in wetlands along the coast, where fresh and salt water mix. The males have one very long, thin, front leg with a claw on it. They use this claw to defend their feeding areas and to fight other males for females during the breeding season. *'Opae 'oeha'a* eat small pieces of rotting plant and animal matter lying on the bottom.

In the olden days, *'opae kala-'ole* and *'opae 'oeha'a*, along with the other stream-climbers, were important food for the Hawaiians, especially during the winter when seas were rough and the men could not go out to fish. During these times, streams became like natural refrigerators for the Hawaiian people, supplying them with high-quality food.

'Opae 'oeha'a Large-clawed Prawn

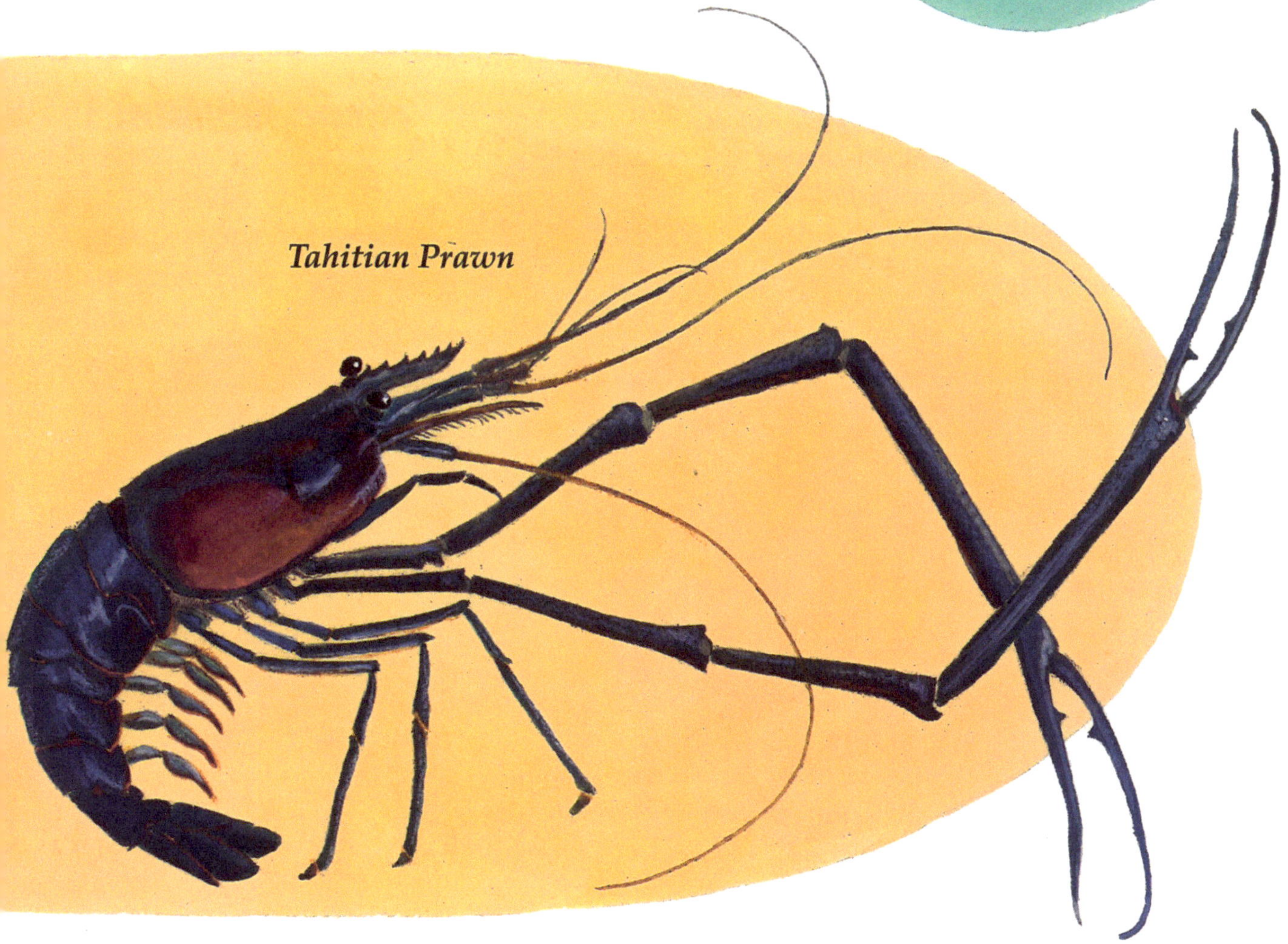

Tahitian Prawn

21

Climbing Snails

Hīhīwai, or *wi*, is the Hawaiian name given to a group of snails that were an important Hawaiian food. The *hīhīwai* with a black shell lives in fast-flowing streams, often high in the mountains. During the day, it rests on the sides and undersides of rocks in white-water areas (rapids and waterfalls). At night, it climbs up the rocks to feed. *Hīhīwai* cling to lava rocks and eat algae from the rock surface. They usually grow up to two inches wide, but those on Molokai sometimes grow much larger.

Female *hīhīwai* lay masses of eggs on rocks and the shells of other *hīhīwai*. When the young hatch, they are washed quickly to sea, where they drift in the plankton. Many months later, the young *hīhīwai* return to the streams. They often follow one another in lines, one behind the other, as they move upstream. Sometimes hundreds of black-shelled *hīhīwai*, each less than half the size of a pea, can be seen moving in a line, creeping across rocks and up the face of a waterfall, like a long, black snake.

Another kind of *hīhīwai*, called *hapawai*, has a smooth, brown shell and lives near the mouths of streams where fresh and salt water mix. Their empty shells are often found along the sand where rivers meet the sea.

A hīhīwai's shell may be smooth or rough depending on where it lives. Hīhīwai that live below the first waterfall have rough shells, while those that live higher up the stream have smooth shells. If a smooth-shelled hīhīwai is moved below the first waterfall, its shell will become rough, and vice-versa.

Hīhīwai

shell underside   smooth shell   rough shell

OTHER STREAM WILDLIFE

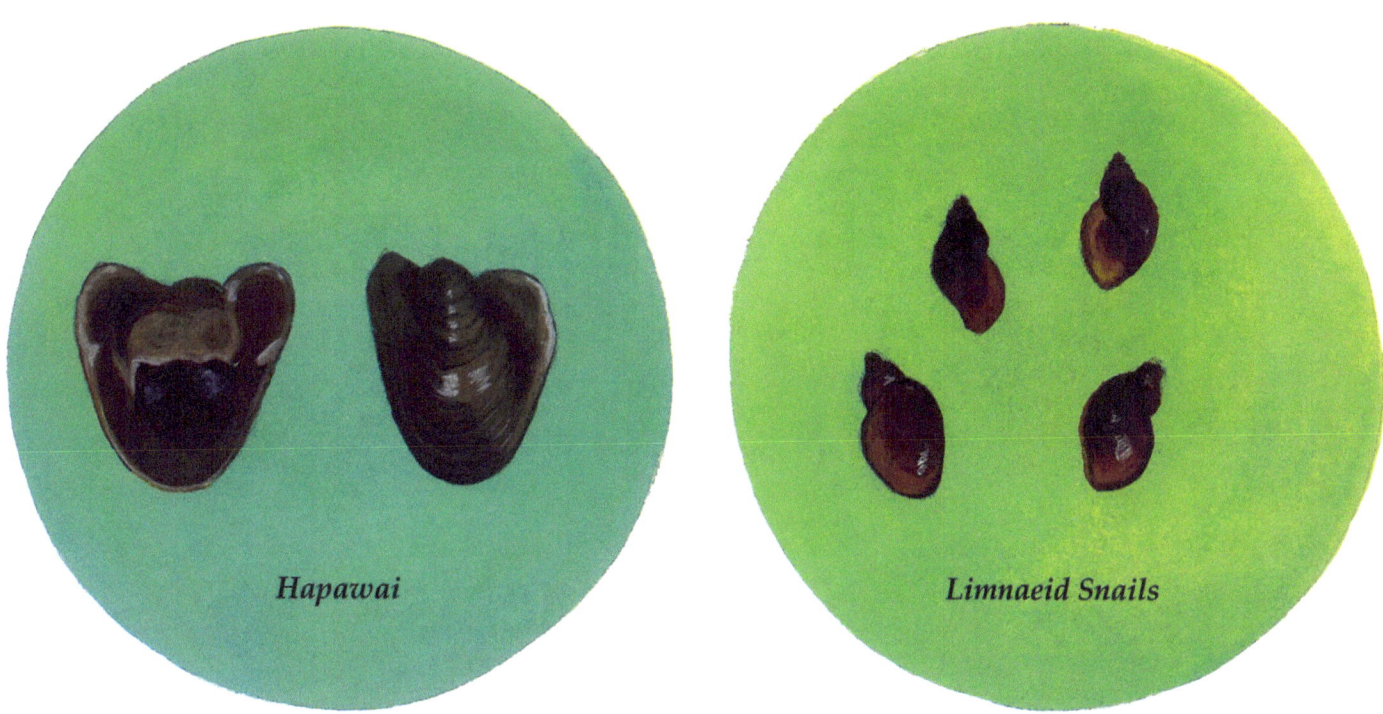

Hapawai　　　　　　　　　　*Limnaeid Snails*

Limnaeid Snails

Limnaeids (lim-NAY-ids) are a group of snails that moved into Hawai'i's streams from land. Their ancestors were land snails that possibly came to Hawai'i with birds—carried in mud that was stuck to their feet or feathers.

Over many generations, limnaeid snails have evolved into many different forms. Some of Hawai'i's limnaeids still live on land. Others have been able to move into streams because they carry a bubble of air inside their shell. Like tiny divers, they carry their air supply with them as they feed underwater.

Some limnaeid snails lay their eggs underwater. Since all limnaeids have both male and female parts, two mating limnaeids fertilize each other's eggs with sperm. Then each snail lays between ten and twenty jelly-like eggs. About five days later, the eggs hatch. The young do not wash downstream, but creep out of the eggs looking like small adults.

One kind of limnaeid snail is found only beside waterfalls. Another kind lives only in streams beneath rotting leaves. As scientists explore further, they will certainly find more types of limnaeids, and discover new things about how they live in Hawai'i's streams.

Dragonfly larva

Adult dragonfly

Adult midge
Midge larva

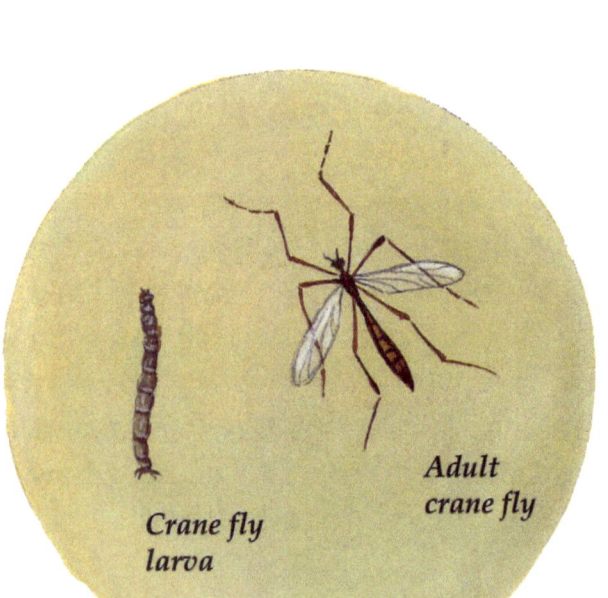
Crane fly larva
Adult crane fly

Insects

Some stream insects, such as beetles, live in fresh water all their lives. Others, such as dragonflies, damselflies, crane flies, and midges, live in fresh water only while they are young. Young midges and crane flies are worm-like, and live along the stream bottom. When they are old enough, the larvae crawl from the water and turn into air-breathing, flying, adults. Adult midges and the much larger crane flies look like mosquitoes, but—happily—they don't bite. Adult midges are important food for damselflies and dragonflies, while midge larvae and adult crane flies are important food for *'o'opu*.

Dragonflies and damselflies, both called *pinao* in Hawaiian, have larvae that live underwater and catch stream insects for food. When *pinao* larvae are old

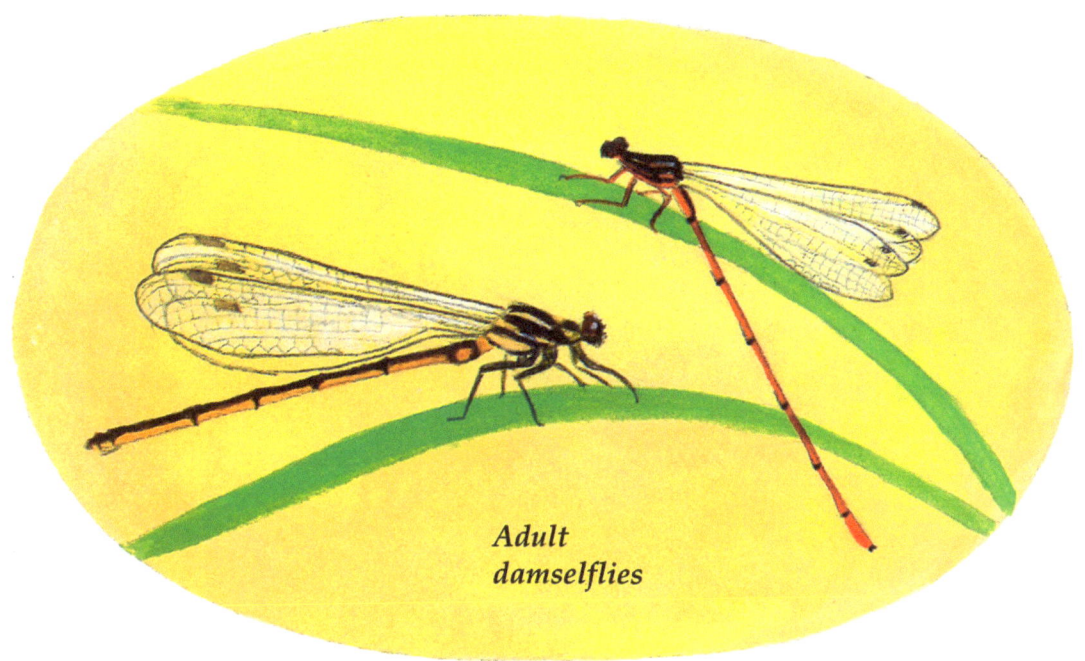

Adult damselflies

Damselfly larva

enough, they develop wings and live above water.

While many freshwater insects that are common in other countries are not found in Hawai'i at all, other insects, such as the damselfly, have evolved into a variety of forms on the islands. Damselflies arrived in Hawai'i long, long ago. Over millions of years, they evolved into many different forms, each looking slightly different and living in a slightly different way. Some damselflies have young that live only in quiet streams and pools. Others have young that live only in wet stream banks, or only along the edges of waterfalls. Still others have young that live among wet leaves along the forest floor, or in small pockets of water held in certain native plants.

Diving beetle

Mullet

Milk Fish

ESTUARIES

An estuary (ES-choo-air-ee) is the wide mouth of a river, or bay, where sea water and fresh water mix. Most of the animals that live in estuaries can live with widely changing amounts of salt in the water. The gobies *'o'opu nakea*, *'o'opu naniha*, *'o'opu 'akupa* and the brown-shelled snail *hapawai* live here, along with many saltwater fish. Estuaries are nurseries and important feeding grounds for saltwater fish, such as mullet, or *ama'ama*; milk fish, or *awa*; barracuda, or *kaku* and flag-tails, or *aholehole*.

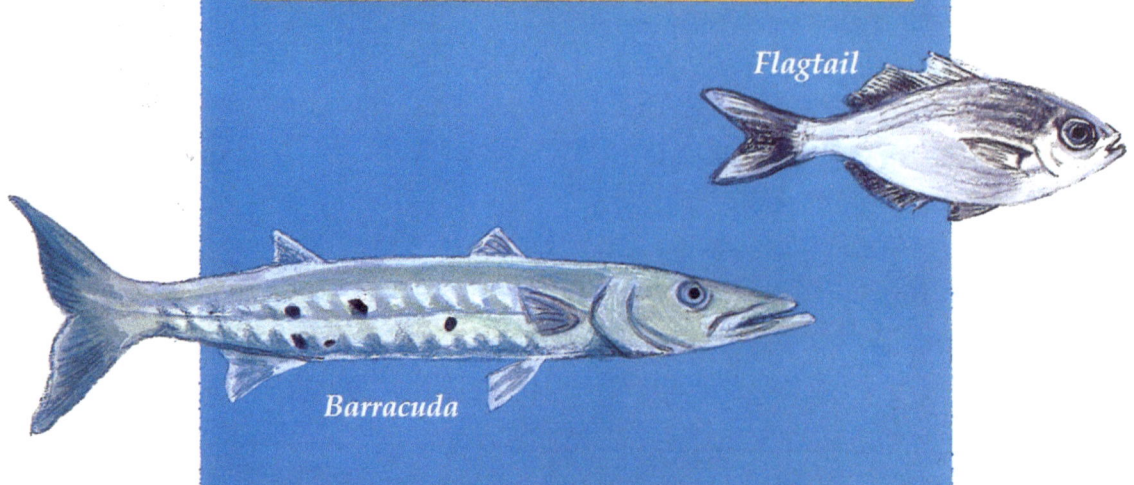

Flagtail

Barracuda

Tilapia

Samoan Crab

Today, most estuaries also contain animals that were brought to Hawai'i by modern man, such as Tahitian prawns, Samoan crabs, and tilapia. Many of these animals were brought here for food. Some have become pests that are replacing native wildlife.

Today's taro farmers create and maintain wetland areas that are used by waterbirds. Taro fields are needed for the survival of Hawaiian ducks, stilts, coots, and gallinules.

WETLANDS

Most of Hawai'i's waterbirds live among the wetlands. Wetlands are usually low, flat lands where rivers and streams flow into the sea. These lands are flooded by water during heavy rains or high tides.

Most of Hawai'i's wetlands have been changed by people. The ancient Hawaiians increased the amount of wetlands through their farming methods. Since 1900, however, wetland areas have shrunk smaller and smaller as people have used the land in other ways. Today, most of Hawai'i's important wetlands are man-made. Ponds, reservoirs, taro fields, drainage ditches, and settling ponds (ponds where wastes from agriculture settle out of the water) are all made and used by people. They are also used—and desperately needed—by Hawai'i's waterbirds. Five of Hawai'i's seven native waterbirds depend on wetlands. So do many shorebirds and waterbirds that migrate to Hawai'i from other lands.

HAWAI'I'S WATERBIRDS

Seven kinds of waterbirds live in Hawai'i. Four of them—the Hawaiian duck, or *koloa*, the Hawaiian gallinule, or *'alae 'ula*, the Hawaiian coot, or *'alae ke'o ke'o*, and the Hawaiian stilt, or *ae'o*,—live only among the wetlands and streams of Hawai'i. As Hawai'i's wetland areas shrink, these birds are in danger of becoming extinct, or disappearing forever. Although they are related to the ducks, coots, gallinules, and stilts found living on the mainland of North America, neither the Hawaiian birds nor the mainland birds fly back and forth. Because they have stayed separate, they have become different over time.

Koloa
Hawaiian duck

The Hawaiian duck, or *koloa*, lives in freshwater areas, from marshes and taro fields to high mountain streams. It eats a variety of foods, including green algae, worms, seeds, some grasses, insects, and snails. Hawaiian ducks feed along the surface of the water and "up-end" their bodies as they reach down to nibble food from the bottom.

Most Hawaiian ducks breed from December through May. During courtship, the male and female fly high into the air, almost straight up, and begin chasing each other in small circles. Having chosen a mate, the female makes her nest on the ground, hiding it among tall grasses, and lining it with soft feathers from her breast. A nest may contain as many as ten pale tan or white eggs, which hatch into fuzzy, light brown or yellow and brown ducklings. After the breeding season, Hawaiian ducks cannot fly for some weeks while they are molting (losing their old feathers and growing new ones). They hide quietly among the marsh grasses until they can fly again.

The Hawaiian stilt, or *ae'o*, can be seen in shallow ponds, taro fields, and mud flats. Unlike the Hawaiian duck and gallinule, Hawaiian stilts are noisy and easy to notice. They wade across shallow water on long, red legs, poking their long bills into the mud to eat worms, insects, fish, and other small animals.

In spring, Hawaiian stilts make their nests on the open ground of small, low islands surrounded by water. The nest is just a shallow bowl scraped into the mud, sometimes with a few short sticks or stones in it. There, the female lays four speckled eggs. Because stilt nests are often on ground that is just a few inches above water level, floods sometimes wipe them out. Yet, if the stilt built a higher nest, it would be easily noticed by predators (animals that would eat the eggs and chicks). If a predator comes too close to the nest or chicks, the parent stilts try to lead it away by calling loudly while bobbing up and down, or by pretending to have a broken wing.

Ae'o
Hawaiian stilt

The Hawaiian gallinule, or *'alae 'ula* has a red bill tipped with yellow. The bill has a large plate that reaches up between the eyes like a flame. Hawaiian legend says this bird brought fire to the Hawaiians, and burned itself as it did so.

The Hawaiian gallinule runs along secret trails among thick weeds in the marsh, choosing to hide rather than fly when it is disturbed. Although its toes are not webbed, it can swim well, chugging through the water as it picks at algae and small insects on and below the surface. Suddenly, the gallinule leaps onto a lily pad and walks among the floating plants. Long, spreading toes keep it from sinking as it turns over one leaf after another, eating small insects and snails it finds on the leaf's underside.

Hawaiian gallinules breed from April through October. They pile marsh plants together to form a shallow nest among thick grass along the water's edge. The female lays between six and thirteen eggs that are light brown with small dark spots. After three weeks, the chicks hatch. Although they leave the nest and swim soon after hatching, they stay close to their mother and find shelter beneath her wings for another few weeks.

'alae 'ula
Hawaiian gallinule

'alae ke'o ke'o
Hawaiian coot

The Hawaiian coot, or *'alae ke'o ke'o* looks a lot like the Hawaiian gallinule, except that its bill is white. Most coots have a white plate between their eyes, but a few coots have a red plate and dark marks near the bill's tip. Coots spend more time in open water than gallinules, and often swim in groups, feeding at the water's surface and diving to eat deeper food. Seeds, insects, snails, fish, and the green parts of water plants are all in the Hawaiian coot's diet. Rounded flaps of skin along their toes help coots dive, swim, and even fly. While in flight, large feet help the bird steer and keep on course.

During the breeding season, April through September, Hawaiian coots build large floating nests among the weeds. They lay four to ten creamy eggs sprinkled with tiny brown specks. Like gallinules, the young coots are able to run and swim almost as soon as they have hatched, but their parents still watch over them for several weeks.

*'Auku'u
Black-crowned
night heron*

The black-crowned night heron, or *'auku'u* feeds among marshes, ponds, streams, and quiet seashores. Night herons aren't usually seen at these places during the day because, unlike other waterbirds, they feed mainly after sunset and before dawn. The heron has sharp eyesight, and hunts frogs, mice, crayfish, snails, and insects by sneaking up on them with its head held low, ready to strike. When hunting for fish, the night heron stands without moving for long moments, waiting to spear a passing fish with its sharp bill. If it gets the chance, a night heron will also snatch the unguarded chicks of other birds.

During the breeding season from April through August, black-crowned night herons nest together in noisy groups. They build large nests of sticks and leaves high in the trees. A female lays up to five bluish green eggs in her nest. After they hatch, the chicks remain in the nest for several weeks, while the parents bring them food.

Hawai'i's black-crowned night herons are the same as the black-crowned night herons found living on the mainlands of North and South America. Since night herons don't fly back and forth between Hawai'i and the mainland, and the two groups don't breed with each other, Hawaiian and mainland night herons will probably become different from each other over time.

Two of Hawai'i's waterbirds do not live among wetlands and streams. The Hawaiian goose, or *nēnē*, is Hawai'i's state bird. Although it is a goose, it no longer lives near water, as its ancestors once did. Today, *nēnē*s live on grassy hillsides and lava flows, from sea level to high mountain slopes. Having lost the need to swim, the *nēnē*'s feet are no longer webbed like those of other geese.

Nēnē Hawaiian goose

Laysan duck

The Laysan duck, which has no Hawaiian name, is only found on Laysan Island, in the Northwest Hawaiian Islands. This is the smallest range, or living area, of any duck in the world. Laysan ducks feed on small flies called brine flies, which rest in large numbers along the sand. When they are disturbed, swarms of brine flies rise into the air. It's a funny sight to see Laysan ducks running down the beach through large clouds of brine flies, snapping up flies with their bills as they go.

Hawaiian ducks, gallinules, coots, stilts, geese, and Laysan ducks are all threatened with extinction (vanishing forever) and are protected by law.

VISITING WATERBIRDS

In mid-August, other waterbirds begin to arrive in Hawai'i's wetlands. They fly to Hawai'i mainly from Canada, Alaska, and Russia, making the long trip to Hawai'i across thousands of miles of open ocean. Pintails, shovellers, American wigeons, green-winged teals, mallards, and lesser scaups are among Hawai'i's winter visitors. Having spent the summer in other countries, breeding and raising their young, these bird come

to Hawai'i for the winter, to rest and feed. Although they don't nest here, these waterbirds depend on Hawai'i's wetlands for their food, shelter, and a place to rest that is free from human disturbance. By April or May, they are ready to fly north again for the summer. As the size of Hawai'i's wetlands decreases, fewer visiting waterbirds come to Hawai'i each year.

WATERBIRDS IN DANGER

There are two main threats to Hawai'i's waterbirds. The first threat is that their habitat, or area where the waterbirds can live, is small and getting smaller. Because wetlands are few, changes there easily harm the birds that depend on them. To protect these waterbirds, many of Hawai'i's remaining wetlands are now protected and cared for as State and National Wildlife Refuges.

Hawai'i's wetlands are shrinking as people destroy marshes to put the land to other uses. Wetlands also shrink as foreign plants, such as California grass, grow over wet areas and make them unusable for waterbirds.

Wildlife Refuge employees and volunteers spend a lot of time removing California grass and other weeds in order to keep the ponds open

Pueo
Hawaiian owl

'Auku'u
Hawaiian Black-crowned
Night Heron

California Grass

for waterbirds. These dedicated people flood and drain man-made mud flats, imitating nature so that small food animals will grow in the mud and provide food for the waterbirds. They build mud islands in ponds to provide nesting sites for Hawaiian stilts, and dig deep water ditches around ponds to keep out cats, dogs, and mongooses, which feed upon the birds and their eggs. At one time, such human activities were not necessary. Today, because humans have changed the nature of Hawai'i's coastlands so much, people must work hard to maintain Hawai'i's wetlands through wise management.

The second major threat to Hawai'i's waterbirds comes from predators. Mongooses, dogs, cats, pigs, rats, cattle egrets, owls, herons, bullfrogs, largemouth bass, and even large toads eat the eggs and chicks of waterbirds. Because most waterbirds nest on the ground, they are easy prey for four-legged hunters. At one time, humans were important predators, too. People shot countless birds for sport and food before killing waterbirds was outlawed in 1939.

Dogs, pigs, rats, mongooses, cats, cattle egrets, largemouth bass, rats, large toads, and bullfrogs eat the eggs and chicks of waterbirds. These animals were all brought to Hawai'i by people.

Waikiki was once a large wetland area.

PEOPLE AND FRESH WATER

As long as people have lived in Hawai'i, they have used Hawai'i's wetlands. The ancient Hawaiians increased wetland areas through farming taro and making fishponds. Later, people also used wetlands to grow rice. More recently, people have destroyed most of Hawai'i's wetlands by draining them to grow sugarcane, and filling them in for building sites. Many homes, hotels, and even cities, now sit on land that was once marsh.

The early Hawaiians managed the land by dividing it into pieces called *ahupua'a* Their plan was based on knowledge that the rain falling in the forested mountains, and the ocean with its reefs full of food fish, were parts of one large system that was connected by flowing rivers and streams. Each river valley, from mountain top to sea, was owned and managed as one piece—one *ahupua'a*. Ditches that took water from a mountain stream to feed crops also returned the water to the same stream. Wetlands were turned into *lo'i*, or taro patches, using water from the streams, and into fishponds by using water from the nearby sea. People were allowed to fish from the sea only in front of the valley where they lived and farmed. By limiting the number of people who could fish or farm any one spot, and practicing a *kapu* system that protected fish from being caught in certain seasons, the ancient Hawaiians practiced wise management, or conservation, of their water and land. The Hawaiians saw their mountains, forests, valleys, streams, and ocean, as sacred and connected— supporting all life. They placed the needs of land and water first, knowing that if they ruined the land and water, they would destroy themselves.

In the last one hundred years, more harm has come to Hawaiian freshwater wildlife than in all the thousands of years that people have called Hawai'i home. Throughout the United States and Europe, people used nature's precious resources to create bigger businesses, more money, and a "better" lifestyle. They began to see nature as something separate from themselves, put there for human use. They saw fresh water, land, rocks, and trees, as resources just waiting to be used. People saw wetlands as wastelands, and natural streams as wasted, unused water.

This attitude toward the land came to Hawai'i in the late 1700s, when Europeans first landed in the islands. Soon the Europeans began taking large amounts of water from streams and moving it from one valley to another to start large-scale farming of sugarcane and pineapples. They used streams as drains to flush away wastes from farming, ranching, and industry. And they used wetlands as dumping grounds for rubbish and as platforms for buildings.

Today, Waikiki is a city.

Today, most Hawaiian streams are dewatered (low in water) because people have taken water from the stream for other uses and not returned it. Dewatered streams are always low in water compared with their natural state. Many stream animals cannot live in dewatered streams because their movement upstream is blocked by lack of water, and because lack of water has changed the stream's natural plant life.

The banks of some streams are regularly sprayed with chemicals to keep them clean of plants that would slow down flood waters. Plants that live along the banks of streams provide food and shade for stream animals. Many insects live among these plants and fall into the streams, becoming more food. Killing or removing plants from the sides of streams removes these sources of food and shade, and allows soil to wash into the stream and onto coral reefs. Poisonous chemicals, oil, and fertilizers seep into streams and wetlands from lawns, golf courses, streets, and roads. These poisons can flow to the sea and pollute the seashore and ocean as well.

We all want to work and play among clean streams, ocean, and shorelines. But chemicals, fertilizers, and other kinds of waste are polluting these places. People like ourselves are causing the damage, and people like ourselves are the ones who decide whether the damage continues or stops.

Today, the lower parts of many Hawaiian streams are dewatered and lined with concrete. Streams lined with concrete can get very hot and kill stream animals, including tiny stream-climbers on their way upstream from the sea. The sides and bottom of a natural stream are as important as its flowing water. Mud, sand, and rocks along the bottom of the stream create living space and food for many stream animals, while plants growing alongside the stream provide cooling shade and more food. These important parts of a stream are removed when a stream is lined with concrete.

NEVER release fish, turtles, or other pets into Hawai'i's streams.

Foreign plants and animals released into streams have replaced native stream animals in many areas. Many marshes have been drained and filled in. For these reasons, most of Hawai'i's native stream and wetland wildlife are becoming fewer in number.

As Hawai'i's human population continues to grow, our use of fresh water increases and the damage to streams and wetlands grows as well. The supply of groundwater (water in the ground used for drinking and washing) has become disturbingly low on some islands. Even Kaua'i, home of the "wettest spot on earth" does not have enough fresh water in its streams and rivers to go around during dry periods.

Introduced species, or plants and animals that are not native to Hawai'i, can harm Hawai'i's freshwater wildlife by eating it or eating its food, by taking over its living space, and by carrying diseases that kill it. Once a new kind of plant or animal produces young, it is very difficult to get rid of.

THE FUTURE IS IN OUR HANDS

The way of thinking that brought such harm to Hawai'i's wetlands and streams in the last one hundred years is changing. Every day, more people are realizing that we are part of nature, and we cannot keep damaging nature without sooner or later destroying ourselves. Like freshwater wildlife, our lives depend on healthy freshwater systems. To live without destroying nature, we must live in balance with it. This means the number of people and their needs must be in balance with what nature can supply to all living things.

People are rediscovering that the peacefulness of birds calling across an open marsh, and the fresh smell of a falling stream that is clean and full of life are an important part of the "better lifestyle" they seek. The value of these healthy natural systems goes beyond money. It is measured in spirit, in joy, and in the sense of well-being that all of us need. As we rediscover the truth that all life is connected, and that streams are really life-lines connecting rainfall in the mountain forests to coral reefs in the sea, we discover the key to sustaining life. We bring back spirit to the land, and find our own spirit as well.

HOW YOU CAN HELP

➤ **DO** become aware of public issues concerning water use and land use.

➤ **Don't** wash liquid containing chemicals down a storm drain. Whatever goes down a storm drain washes directly to the sea. The chemicals can harm corals and other sea life, and can pollute the places where we swim.

➤ **DO** send water into areas with growing plants instead of down storm drains whenever you can.

➤ **Don't** release pet fish into streams and lakes. They may eat the native species or compete with them for food and living space.

➤ **DO** become aware of the items around us that contain harmful chemicals. Car batteries, motor oil, paints and thinners are some of the items that must be disposed of carefully. If you are not sure how to dispose of certain items, check with the Department of Health.

GLOSSARY

algae certain kinds of plants that live in fresh or salt water.

ancestors those people (or animals) from whom (or from which) one is descended, usually living at least a generation before one's grandparents.

conservation prevention of loss, waste, or damage.

courtship special behavior to win the interest of a possible mate.

dewater to remove water from.

estuary the mouth of a river, where salt water and fresh water mix.

evolve to develop and change naturally and gradually.

extinct no longer existing.

generation a single stage or step in family descent. Grandparents, parents, and children are three generations.

habitat the place in nature where plants and animals live. Different habitats provide food and shelter for different kinds of animals.

hatchling an animal that has newly emerged from the egg.

larva, (plural: **larvae**) a young fish or insect in the first stage of its life after coming out of the egg.

marsh wet land that is usually low-lying near the sea.

migrate to move from one place to another. Birds and fish migrate with the seasons.

molt to lose old feathers or fur so that new feathers or fur can grow in.

plankton forms of plant and animal life that drift in lakes, rivers and oceans.

porous allowing water to pass through.

predator an animal that preys upon other animals for food.

range an area throughout which plants are found growing or animals are found living.

taro a tropical plant, the leaves and roots of which are important food.

territorial territorial animals are those which protect a "territory," or area of land or water they regard as belonging to themselves.

INDEX

ae'o 25, 27
ahina 11
aholehole 22
ahupua'a 36
'alae 'ula 25, 28
'alae ke'o ke'o 25, 27, 29
ama'ama 22
American wigeon 32
'auku'u 30, 35
awa 22
barracuda 22
beetles 20
black-crowned night herons 30, 35
brine flies 31
California grass 34, 35
crane flies 20
damselflies 20, 21
dragonflies 20
estuary 22
fishponds 36
flagtail 22
green-winged teal 33
habitat 34, 42
hapawai 19, 22
Hawaiian coot 24, 25, 29, 31
Hawaiian duck 26, 27
Hawaiian gallinule 28
Hawaiian goose 31
Hawaiian stilt 27
hīhīwai 18
hinana 11
kaku 22
kapu 37
koloa 25, 26

Kona storms 4
Laysan duck 31
Laysan Island 31
lesser scaup 33
limnaeid snails 19
limu 10
lo'i 36
mallard 33
marsh 3, 26, 28, 30, 34, 36, 39, 40, 42
midges 20
milk fish 22
mountain shrimp 16
mullet 22
nēnē 31
'o'opu 'akupa 15, 22
'o'opu 'alamo'o 12, 13
'o'opu nakea 7, 8, 10, 12
'o'opu naniha 15, 22
'o'opu nopili 14
'ōpae kala-'ole 16, 17
pinao 20
Pintail 32
plankton 11, 16
rice 36
Samoan crab 23
shoveller 32
sugarcane 36, 37
Tahitian prawn 16, 17
taro 26
Tilapia 23
Trade Winds 4
wetlands 24
wi 18

www.ingramcontent.com/pod-product-compliance
Lightning Source LLC
Chambersburg PA
CBHW041120300426
44112CB00002B/43